HEADstart

FLAGS

First published in Great Britain by
CAXTON EDITIONS
an imprint of
The Caxton Book Company,
16 Connaught Street,
Marble Arch, London, W2 2AF.

Due to the printing process, the colour of the flags in this book may not always reflect the
exact colour of the genuine flag.

ISBN 1 84067 021 5

A copy of the CIP data for this book is available from the British Library upon request.

With grateful thanks to Helen Courtney

Created and produced for Caxton Editions by
FLAME TREE PUBLISHING,
a part of The Foundry Creative Media Company Ltd,
Crabtree Hall, Crabtree Lane,
Fulham, London, SW6 6TY.

Printed in Singapore by Star Standard Industries Pte. Ltd.

HEADstart

FLAGS

*The Flags of the World's
Nations Explained in
Glorious Colour*

MAUREEN HILL

CAXTON EDITIONS

Contents

Introduction

The study of flags is called 'vexillology'. This name comes from the Ancient Roman name for a flag, 'vexillum'.

Flags have been important all over the world for about 5,000 years. Today, flags are used to represent groups of people such as an army regiment, a troop of Boys Scouts or Brownies, or a school. National flags represent an entire country and some flags represent groups of countries, like the United Nations. Flags are flown to mark important events like coronations and are flown at 'half-mast', half way up the flagpole, to honour the dead.

Banners, standards, pennants and colours are other names for flags. Most flags nowadays are rectangular in shape, but they do not have to be.

Flags were first used as symbols to identify families or groups of people. During the Middle Ages, knights fixed pennants to their lances to help identify them from their enemies.

In Europe, during the Middle Ages, a new system of 'heraldry' set down strict rules about what could be put on individual families' coats of arms and flags. These rules have affected the designs on many Western flags of today.

There are special words used to describe the various parts of a flag. The side of the flag that

faces the viewer when the flagpole is on the left is called the 'obverse', the other side the 'reverse'. The 'hoist' is the side of the flag next to the flagpole; the side away from the pole is called the 'fly'. 'Canton' is the word for the four quarters into which the flag is divided.

National Flags

When most people think of flags they think of the flags that represent the various countries of the world. These national flags are usually very important in a country's life. National flags will often represent a country's history or say something about its religion or beliefs.

The flag of the Northern Marianas shows its history, geography and its relationship with the USA. On a blue background that represents the Pacific Ocean there is a grey 'chalice', or cup, that symbolizes the ancient civilization of the islands. Over the top of the chalice is a white star that represents the islands' position as part of the Commonwealth of the USA.

Many Christian countries have crosses on their national flags. Islamic countries often include the crescent moon symbol. The colours of the flag can also be important. Green is the colour associated with Islam, while red is the colour associated with Communism. China's flag has a red background with a large gold star which stands for Communism, and four smaller stars that represent the four social classes of the country.

National flags are often very important symbols of a country and something for its people to take pride in.

Flags of the Countries of the European Union

The European Union (EU) is made up of 15 countries – Austria, Belgium, Denmark, Finland, France, Germany, Great Britain, Greece, Ireland, Italy, Luxembourg, the Netherlands, Portugal, Spain and Sweden.

Red, black and gold appear on both the German and Belgian flags, but they look very different. The flag of Belgium is much squarer than most national flags and the colours are arranged in vertical stripes. The German flag's colours are in horizontal stripes. The colours in the flag have very strong associations with the unity of Germany, and when Germany was divided into East and West, both sides used the same basic flag.

France's flag is known as the 'Tricolour'. It was first flown during the French Revolution and the colours are thought to be red and blue to represent Paris, together with the white of the royal flag.

The design of the Italian flag is probably based on that of France's Tricolour. The Frenchman Napoleon ruled Italy for a number of years and his standard was based on the French flag.

Ireland's flag is a symbol of hope. The green of the flag represents the Catholic majority in Ireland, the orange the Protestant minority and the white symbolizes the peace between them.

Flags of Europe

The EU (European Union) represents a large majority of the countries that used to be known as Western Europe. Norway and Switzerland are exceptions to this.

Switzerland's flag, which was first used as a national flag in 1848, is thought to date back to the thirteenth or fourteenth century when Swiss soldiers wore the 'Holy Cross'. The flag of the International Red Cross is based on the Swiss flag, except the colours are reversed. The founder of the Red Cross, Jean Henri Dunant, was Swiss.

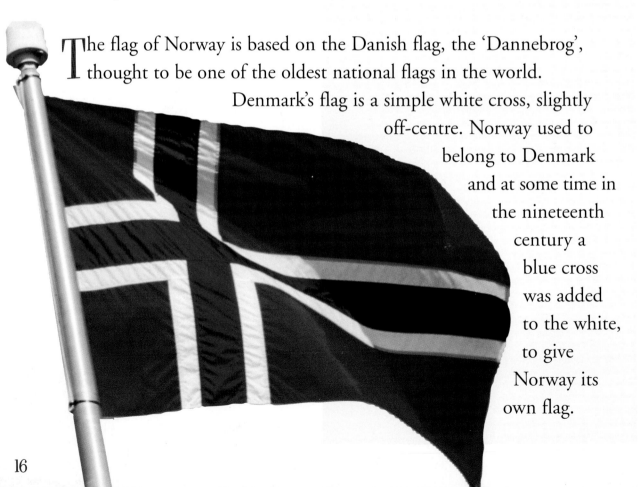

The flag of Norway is based on the Danish flag, the 'Dannebrog', thought to be one of the oldest national flags in the world. Denmark's flag is a simple white cross, slightly off-centre. Norway used to belong to Denmark and at some time in the nineteenth century a blue cross was added to the white, to give Norway its own flag.

Many of the countries that were in Eastern Europe have made changes to their flags to reflect the political changes since the fall of Communism in 1989.

Poland's flag was developed from an ancient coat of arms showing a white eagle on a red background. The current flag (right) was first used in 1918 and throughout Poland's troubled history in the twentieth century the flag has remained the same.

Hungary's flag has had some minor changes made to it over the years since it was first used in 1848. The red, white and green colours of the flag date back to the ninth century but the design of the flag was influenced by the French Tricolour.

The Union Jack

The Union Jack is the flag of the United Kingdom of Great Britain and Northern Ireland. Its official name is the British Union Flag.

The Union Jack was first used as a national flag in 1707. This flag symbolized the Union of the Parliament of Scotland with the Parliament that governed England and Wales. Although the countries had shared the same monarch since 1603 they were not really one country. The Act of Union in 1707 joined them together to make Great Britain. The joint flag was a

combintion of the flags of England and Scotland. The English flag – the red cross of St George on a white background – dates back to the thirteenth century. The white diagonal, or 'saltire', cross of St Andrew on a blue back-ground appears on the flag of Scotland.

In 1801, a second Act of Union united Great Britain with Ireland and the red saltire cross of St Patrick was laid into the white cross of St Andrew. When a large part of Ireland became the independent state of Eire in 1937, the Union Jack did not change. The St Patrick's flag now repre-sents the six counties in Northern Ireland, often called Ulster.

The Stars and Stripes

The 'Stars and Stripes' is one of the nicknames for the flag of the United States of America. It is also known as the 'Star-Spangled Banner', the 'Red, White and Blue', 'Old Glory' or just simply the 'American flag'.

The colours on the American flag reflect the fact that the USA was once a British colony, but they are also symbolic of American values. The white stands for purity and innocence, the red for hardiness and valour and the blue for vigilance, perseverance and justice.

In 1777, the American Congress, or Parliament, announced that there would be a new flag: 'The flag of the United States shall be 13 stripes, alternate red and white, with a union of 13 stars on a blue field.'

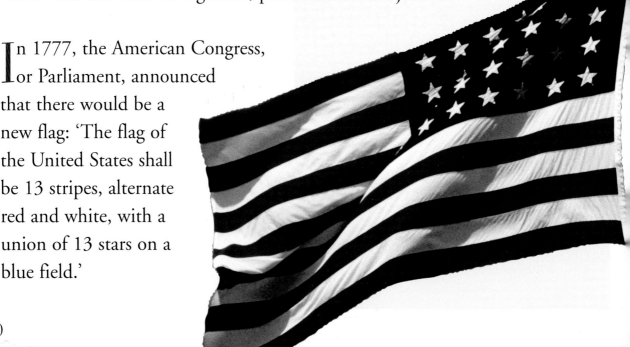

EXCELSIOR

The 13 stars and stripes were to represent the 13 states which made up the original United States of America. In the early flags the stars were often displayed in a circle. Sometimes 12 of the stars were shown in a circle around a large one in the middle.

As the number of states in the Union increased there was a demand that all the states be represented on the flag. Congress agreed that, for every new state, a new star should be added to the flag.

The present American flag has 50 stars, the last two were added in 1959 and 1960, for Alaska and Hawaii. The stripes have never been changed and remain at 13 to symbolize the original states of the United States of America.

Each of the 50 states which make up the USA also has its own flag. The flag of New York is shown above.

Flags from Africa

Many African nations have been independent for less than 50 years. Their flags are often very carefully designed to represent both the country and the beliefs of its people.

Liberia has been an independent country since 1847. Most of the people who founded Liberia were freed slaves from the USA and this influenced the design of the flag. The flag's 11 stripes stand for the men who signed the bill of independence. The blue background, or 'field', stands for Africa and the single star represents a free and independent nation.

Some African countries had to struggle for independence. In Zambia, the colours of the political party that led the fight for independence became the colours of the national flag. The eagle stands for freedom and the colours are also symbolic. The green field is for farming, black for the people, red for the blood spilled in the fight for freedom, and orange for the country's minerals, mainly copper.

Malawi did not have the same violent struggle for independence as Zambia, but it too adopted the colours of its main political party. The red, black and green are symbolic colours throughout Africa and stand for the struggle for freedom. The rising sun was added to represent the beginning of a new era.

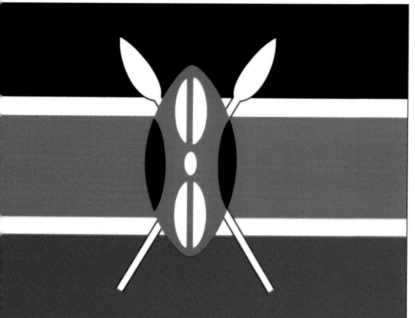

Horizontal black, red and green stripes also appear on the Kenyan flag. To these are added two thin white stripes to represent peace. In the centre of the flag are the shield and spear of a Masai warrior, indicating the defence of freedom and the history and culture of the people.

The flag of the Gambia is very simple. The red stands for the sun, the blue for the River Gambia and the green for farming. The white stripes symbolize peace.

Flags of Island Nations

In the Pacific and Indian Oceans are many nations made up either of single islands or groups of islands. These nations' flags often display symbols that reflect their island homes.

Kiribati is an independent nation consisting of 33 small islands. It has a beautiful flag that reflects the environment of the islands. The flag shows the Pacific Ocean with the sun rising over it. Above the sun is a frigate bird that breeds on the islands and flies over the ocean in search of food.

The Marshall Islands also have a striking flag. Again the ocean is represented, this time as a blue field. The position of the star shows the country's position in relation to the equator, which is symbolized by the orange and white line. In the line the white stands for brightness and the orange for courage.

The state of Nauru is composed of only one island. Its flag is similar to that of the Marshall Islands in that the star represents the island's position in relation to the equator, shown as a thin yellow stripe. The 12 points on the star represent the 12 tribes on the island.

St Lucia is in the Caribbean Sea and its flag has a blue field to represent that fact. The triangle in the middle stands for the land, the colour black represents the volcanoes on the island and the yellow is for the golden sands of the beaches.

National Flags with Religious Symbols

For centuries flags have been used by the worlds' religions. Many of the symbols associated with those religions appear on the flags of various nations. The Union Jack is a group of religious crosses representing the patron saints of the member countries.

Saudi Arabia is the home of the holiest shrines of Islam. The country's flag is green, the colour of Islam. On the green field are the sword of authority

and an inscription in Arabic. The words read: 'There is no God but Allah and Mohammed is the Prophet of Allah'. The flag is a double flag, which means that the inscription can be read from both sides.

The Vatican City State is a tiny country within the city of Rome. It is an independent country that is home to the Pope, the leader of the Roman Catholic religion. The Vatican flag is white and yellow which are traditional colours associated with the Pope. The flag also carries the Vatican's coat of arms which shows the keys of heaven and the Pope's hat.

On the flag of Bhutan the orange-red colour represents the Buddhist religion. Bhutan is a kingdom in the Himalayas and the royal power is symbolized by the orange-yellow. Bhutan means 'Land of the Dragon' and so the dragon is also shown on the flag.

The present state of Israel came into being in 1948 as a homeland for Jewish people all over the world. Israel's flag is based on the 'tallith', a traditional prayer shawl. At the centre of the flag is one of Judaism's most important symbols, the Star of David.

International Flags

The United Nations (UN) is based in New York but it is made up of nearly all the countries in the world. The United Nation's flag is a map of the world as it looks from the North Pole. The world is surrounded by olive branches which are traditional symbols of peace. The blue background has become an important colour to symbolize peace throughout the world. When soldiers from the countries that make up the UN are sent in to help keep the peace in parts of the world where there is fighting, they wear blue berets and paint some of their equipment blue.

Besides the UN, which represents the whole world, there are other groups of countries that have combined together. In Europe, the European Union consists of 15 countries, each with their own national flag. The EU flag is very simple. It has a dark blue field on which are 15 stars in a circle. Each star represents one of the member countries and the circle symbolizes their unity.

The Organisation of African Unity is made up of many African nations. The combination of colours on the Organisation's flag was deliberately chosen to be unlike those of any of the member states. In the centre of the flag is a map of Africa surrounded by olive branches.

Many international flags represent political groups but the flag of the International Olympics is concerned with peaceful competition through sport. The Olympic flag consists of different coloured rings linked together. Each of the rings represents one of the five continents of the world.

Unusual National Flags

Most flags are rectangular in shape. The flag of Nepal is the most unusually shaped of all national flags. Two triangular pennants were joined together in the nineteenth century to make one flag. The symbols on the flag of the sun and the moon reflect the idea that Nepal should be everlasting.

The flag of Libya is unusual because it is very plain. But the single-coloured green flag with no emblems still has meaning. The green represents both the Islamic religion of the nation and the hope for a 'green revolution' to feed the people.

The colour of the flag of Qatar, a country on the Persian Gulf, is the result of an accident. Originally the flag was supposed to be red and white. In the very bright sunlight of Qatar the red turned maroon. The maroon was eventually accepted as the official colour.

Grenada, an island in the West Indies, has a colourful flag with an unusual and complex design. The most unusual element of this flag is the inclusion of an emblem of a nutmeg. The country's economy relies on the growing of nutmegs.

Flags with Emblems in the Middle

The colours in a flag are always important and many flags are made up of colours in geometric designs, where both the colours and the shapes mean different things. However, many flags include important national emblems, often in the centre of the flag.

The flag of Japan is very striking and very simple. The emblem in the centre is from ancient Japanese heraldry and represents the sun. Japan is called the 'Land of the Rising Sun' and its emperor was traditionally believed to be descended from the sun.

The Canadian flag was designed in 1964 and first flown the following year. Red and white are the country's national colours. At the centre of the flag is the maple leaf emblem. The maple leaf has been a symbol of freedom for many years. The maple tree gives a sweet syrup. In the eighteenth and nineteenth centuries this was a way of having a sweetener without having to use sugar grown using slave labour in the plantations of America or the West Indies.

Cambodia (sometimes called Kampuchea) has had a very violent history and the flag has changed many times. Throughout all the changes the emblem in the middle has always stayed the same. The emblem shows the ancient Hindu temple of Angkor Wat.

Another country with a troubled history is Lebanon. It also includes on its flag an ancient symbol. The cedar tree has been associated with Lebanon since the days of the Bible.

Changing Flags

Sometimes war or politics bring change to a country. Usually the country's flag is changed to reflect this. In recent years, many events have occurred in different countries across the world. A great many of these changes have been due to the fall of Communism in Russia and Eastern Europe.

The old flag of the USSR was red, with a star and a hammer and 'sickle', a tool for cutting crops, which represented workers in industry and on farms. The Union of Soviet Socialist Republics was a group of 15 republics ruled by the Communist party. The Union broke up in 1989 when the Communists lost power. Each republic became a country on its own and chose a new flag.

Georgia is one of those countries. Its dark red, black and white flag was first used in 1918. Unfortunately, Georgia only remained a free country for three years before it became part of the USSR. When it again became free it chose to have the same flag.

Russia, the largest republic, chose a white, blue and red flag. Russia's flag is very similar to that of Slovakia. Slovakia was joined to the Czech Republic and the two countries became Czechoslovakia between 1918 and 1993. It was also ruled by the Communists. The two countries' flags use the traditional colours associated with the people of the area but the Slovakian flags includes an ancient crest.

South Africa is another country that has seen great political change in the 1990s. The old South African flag represented only the Europeans that lived there, and the Dutch, or 'Boer' settlers in particular. The majority of the population of South Africa was not represented. The new flag (below) represents everyone and each individual is supposed to make their own meaning from its design.

Military Flags

Many flags started off as symbols to represent countries or groups of people in battle. Today the armies, navies and airforces of all countries have their own flags. These flags are called 'ensigns'. Within each army or airforce, each regiment or squadron has its own flag.

The British Royal Navy flies the white ensign, which is a white flag with a red cross and a Union Jack in the top left quarter or 'canton'.

The Union Jack in the canton appears on both the British Army and the British Royal Airforce (RAF) flags. A series of red, white and blue circles arranged rather like a target, appears on the RAF ensign. It is an official symbol of the RAF and can be seen painted on the side of RAF aeroplanes.

On the Army ensign is an emblem of crossed swords, a reminder of the time many years ago when armies fought with swords. The crown and lion are symbols of the British Queen or King who is always the Army's commander-in-chief.

Many of the regimental flags belonging to European armies developed from the idea of heraldry and are often very elaborate. The colour of the field of a regimental flag often reflects the colour of the original regimental uniform.

Flags in History

The first flags were probably used in ancient China and India. The idea of a flag is thought to have developed from streamers that were attached to poles with symbolic carvings. The ancient Egyptians used these poles. Flags are mentioned in the Bible and we know that both the Greeks and Romans used them.

The American War of Independence and the American Civil War produced many interesting flags. Washington's Guard was a regiment made up of men from many of the different regiments fighting against Britain in the War of Independence. Interestingly, this flag included a depiction of an eagle, which was later to become the emblem of the USA.

During the American Civil War in the nineteenth century, many different regiments were formed on both sides. The Confederate States of America, often simply called the South, produced its own flags. The most well known is probably the battle flag, a blue diagonal cross on a red background. Inside the cross are 13 stars to represent the states in the confederacy.

The other side in the Civil War was usually referred to as the North or the Union. It, too, produced many beautiful flags. The state of New York has 1,000 flags from the Civil War. The North was richer than the South and many of these flags were made of silk. Silk does not keep as well as the cotton or wool that the Southern flags were made of. Many of the flags of the North are now falling apart, while a lot of the flags from the South have lasted.

Signal Flags

Flags are a means of communication. They communicate belonging to a group or a country. They can also communicate distress when flown upside down. Flags are dipped in salute and are flown at half-mast as a sign of mourning.

Flags can be used to communicate more direct messages. Ships fly the Blue Peter as a signal that they are about to sail. A half red and half white flag signals that a pilot is on board the ship.

There is an international flag code that has been used on ships since 1857. In this code each flag stands for a letter or a number, but each flag also has its own unique meaning. For example the red and white flag that signals a pilot is on board is also the signal flag for the letter H. The plain yellow flag stands for the letter Q but when it is flown on its own it means that there is plague on board. The O flag means man overboard and D means a ship is having difficulty steering. Sailors today still have to learn this signal code.

Semaphore is another signal system using flags. In semaphore it is not the flags themselves that carry the signal but the positions in which they are placed.

Children's Flags

Many children's organisations and institutions have their own flags.

Schools often have their own flags that are flown on special days either for the school or the country. Usually, the school flag will be in the school uniform colours and include the school crest or badge.

Many youth and children's organisations around the world have their own flags. The Scout and Guide Movement uses flags. Each unit will have its own flag. There are also flags, like the World Scout flag, that represent the international organisation.

UNICEF, the United Nation's Children's Fund, is an organisation which represents children and tries to make life better for all children in the world.

Flag Days

Charities often raise funds by selling 'flags' of their charities' emblem. Originally they were small fabric or paper flags that were attached by pins. Nowadays most 'flags' are paper with self-adhesive backs. Charities like the Royal National Lifeboat Institute (RNLI), the St John's Ambulance Brigade and the Red Cross all hold flag days.

Further Information

Places to Visit

National Army Museum - includes regimental colours and battle flags. The National Army Museum, Royal Hospital Road, Chelsea, London, SW3 4HT. Telephone: 0171 730 0717.

Commonwealth Institute - see flags and cultures of the 54 countries that are members of the British Commonwealth. The Commonwealth Institute, Kensington High Street, London, W8. Telephone: 0171 603 4535.

The National Maritime Museum - naval flags amongst paintings and the history of British seafaring. The National Maritime Museum, Park Row, Greenwich, London, SE10 9NF. Telephone: 0181 858 4422.

Trooping the Colour - annual event around the time of the Queen's official birthday. Takes place in Horse Guards Parade.

Further Reading

I-Spy Flags I-Spy Ltd. - book of almost 200 national flags arranged in alphabetical order. Score points every time you spot one.

Web Sites

The Flag Institute Web Page - http://www.flaginst.demon.co.uk/vexillolgy.html for discussions and updates about flags.

Picture Credits

All pictures courtesy of Foundry Arts except:
Image Select: pp. 10
Salamander: pp. 39
Topham Picturepoint: pp. 8, 15, 16, 17, 18, 19, 20, 23, 31, 38, 40, 41, 43
Visual Arts Library: pp. 11